Team Wave SURFING

RULES BOOK 2018

BY
TEAM WAVE SURFING
NON-PROFIT

COPYRIGHTS

TABLE OF CONTENTS

DEDICATION

The idea of Team Wave Surfing was created by parents who wanted their kids to find other kids to learn to surf with and to play with in the same manner as other team sports like soccer, lacrosse and football. The passion to create an environment for our kids was important to each of us. We dedicate this Team Wave Surfing book to the Island of Hawaii and the surfers who continue to share in the art of surfing.

ACKNOWLEDGMENTS

We'd like to thank Steve Cassell for collaborating with us to create this sport. Working on this and tuning the idea of an interactive game in surfing was one of the most exciting endeavors we have taken on as a family and we appreciate the time spent at the Young Eagles with Steve and Suzy while our kids learned to fly, and we birthed a dream.

CHAPTER 1. INTRODUCTION TO THE SPORT OF TEAM SURFING

TEAM WAVE SURFING was born with youth and unity in mind. Three parents started it all when sitting at the beach and complaining about their children not having any other kids with whom they could surf. The parents turned to their son, a college level athlete with years of competitive sports experience, for inspiration on how to make team surfing a possibility. Surfing has lacked the collaboration and unity that set other mainstream sports apart. There was no game play where kids could learn the sport, enjoy meeting new friends, and comfortably work together. Currently, kids couldn't support one another without jeopardizing their own success. Surfing needed a different path that would jumpstart a new generation of surf supporters. There needed to be an environment that provided young surfers a way to connect with each other.

Those same three parents thought: why can't we create a team-orientated sport for budding and inexperienced surfers? Why can't we shift the sport of surfing from being solo-focused? And why can't we create something new and make surfing a team based endeavor?

In that moment, **TEAM WAVE SURFING** became reality. **TEAM WAVE SURFING** is an inventive, fun, and interactive game that has multiple players working as a single unit to catch and ride the wave.

CHAPTER 2. PURPOSE AND SCOPE OF TEAM WAVE SURFING RULE BOOK

The Team Wave Surfing rule book outlines the official requirements, regulations, scoring, and dynamics that are essential to creating the unique experience of team wave surfing. This rule book is to be launched as a guideline for a youth surf division and could grow to reach the professional level in the future. The sport outlined in this document will grab young surfers with its constant competition, suspense, action, team play, cohesiveness, and spotlighting capabilities.

The rulebook will clearly state the definition of the game, the mission of the game play, the players, judging, and overall basis for the sport.

CHAPTER 3. THE GAME OF TEAM WAVE SURFING

Three Players per Heap

The game of TEAM WAVE SURFING will involve two teams of 6-12 total players with rounds of fifteen minutes for four heaps. An additional heap, or quarter play time, may be initiated in the case of a tie. In each heap, three players from each team compete to ride the most waves for the longest amount of time, one by one with the goal to stay on that wave together.

A coin toss led by the referees initiates the start of the game. The team captain from both teams participates to determine who gets first priority in the round. First priority, which is the time the team 'owns' that wave line, is switched after each heap. There is a five-minute break between each heap for substitutions and a ten-minute halftime.

As a team based sport, points are gained by a team's ability to catch and maneuver the series of waves on the wave line for their play time, stay on that wave line together, do tricks together and play together. Players constantly compete for wave time and priority during the heap.

The teams can earn additional points for having multiple players on a wave during the same time. Additional points are awarded at the end of each heap for the team with the longest time spent on a wave. Teamwork is what earns the most points.

Judges, a timekeeper, wave timekeeper, flagger, and a referee manage the game play, adhere to the rules, and collectively identify points, fouls, and off-sides for the players.

Team wave surfing is about team work, surfing, and fun.

CHAPTER 4. WHAT IS TEAM SURFING AND HOW WILL IT CHANGE THE FACE OF SURFING

Team Wave Surfing hopes to add to the sport of surfing by: complementing it from a traditional one-person centered sport, to a team based, team building sport of unity.

It will be used to cohesively unite youth interest in the sport of surfing overall while creating a new cutting edge, suspenseful, high energy and exciting team sport to be played all over the world.

Seasoned and amateur surfers of all ages can enjoy the game, bringing a new level of comradery and fun to their day of surfing.

Youth that may not have been interested in the sport as a solo competitor can now enjoy the sport as a part of the team, regardless of their skill level.

Team Wave Surfing isn't about being the one best surfer; it's about being a great team.

Chapter 5

CHAPTER 5. TEAM WAVE SURFING CONSTITUTION

Each League-endorsed team formed within the Team Wave Surfing League must have a constitution. The constitution will outline the below makeup of the member club.

1. Adopted date: Date the club was started.
2. Name: Your team's official name and the name of the sports club.
3. Purpose: The reason the team or sports club was formed.
4. Membership: Outlines who can qualify for membership as a full member, guest member, and the rights or honors of either.
5. Meetings: Notes how many meetings, recording of meetings, and definition of meetings to be held.
6. Elections: This should outline the way in which elections will take place, the rules for the elections, and time frame for elections.
7. Executive Board: This will specify the guiding body of officers that will be in leadership, the duration, the limited number of times a person can hold office.
8. Funding: The method in which the team plans to gain funding for the sport, and for membership.
9. Divisions: Description of what divisions and committees should be formed to support the league.
10. Affiliations: This section should note the various local or state affiliations and ruling bodies.
11. Advisor: The board of Team Wave Surfing will serve as advisor to the leagues managing the sport.
12. Coach: Each coach and manager of the team should undergo background checks, recording of the validation and their tasks should be outlined.
13. Ratification Procedures: This will specify how changes to the constitution for the

league will be modified, updated, or re-written. Also, noting the persons to sign off of such changes.

14. Bylaws: Will state what rules and regulations are for each participating team within the league.

CHAPTER 6. PLAYING GAME LOCATION

The game location is preferable in an ocean with a wide enough wave line to accommodate three players from each team on one wave.

A. BEACH: Team Wave Surfing is meant to be played on a beach, in a wave, or in a state-of-the-art wave pool that can accommodate the full number of team players needed for a heap.

B. WAVE LINE: Each team should spread itself in key positions to catch the entire wave line at various points as a team within the 15 minutes of each heap. There will be several waves to be ridden on the wave line during the priority time. For maximum use of play area, the team should seek and maximize all opportunities to capture and ride the wave on the wave line. They are given 5 minutes to set up.

C. OCEAN: The preferable location is in the ocean where there are waves present that can accommodate multiple players.

NOTE: BUOYS are placed in TAKE OFF ZONES that designates the off-sides locations for penalty.

D. STATE (IN USA): The sport's initial location of inception will be Oahu, HI with hopes of expanding to other locations in the United States.

E. INTERNATIONAL LOCATIONS (PROPOSED): The hope is that eventually this will be a sport enjoyed at the international level.

F. EVENT LICENSEE will have the notice and approval at the judges table.

G. INSURANCE for each team has to be in place and proof provided to the head judge upon starting game or that team will forfeit game.

Chapter 7

CHAPTER 7. OVERVIEW OF HOW TO PLAY THE GAME OF TEAM WAVE SURFING

This overview will give a broad view of the actions that take place during the game and will put in perspective how to play the game. Please review the sections below regarding rules, points, and penalties.

PHASES OF THE GAME	
Playing Area	• The wave line consists of a succession of waves that are available for capture during a team's priority time on the wave. The priority is determined by the Front Rider team member's decision to take the wave opportunity on the wave line. The time for that team to capture play opportunity is during their 15 minute play time.
Coin Toss	• Team captain who wins the toss decides 1st priority for the 1st HEAP. After HEAP 1, each team takes turns in switching of priority with no coin toss necessary.
Heap 1: 15 minutes of play THE SETUP	• Three heap players from each team take a place on the wave line. • A coach from each team can be in the water to facilitate plays but they must be off-sides and out of the way of the game play areas.

Heap 1: 15 minutes of play
GAME PLAY

• One of the team members that won the initial coin toss sets the priority by taking the first wave chosen within the first two minutes of play. Once a team member assumes the role as the 1st Front Rider, priority is established for the team.

• If priority isn't claimed in first five minutes, it switches to the opposing team.

• The team with priority has each player after the Front Rider take the wave at their opportune time. The Middle Rider will follow the Front Rider onto the wave, then the Wing Man or Wild Card rider will either 'save' a play by dropping in where the Front Rider or Middle Rider lost their place or will close the play.

• When Team 1 is finished their priority time, the priority is then switched to the opposing team.

• Players may gain points by (1) riding a wave according to rules in this rule book, (2) having more than one player from the same team on a wave at a time, (3) doing tricks on the wave, (4) doing coordinated tricks on the wave, (5) having their team stay on the wave the longest time.

• Substitutions may be made according to the rules outlined below.

Break - 5 minute substitution time

Heap 2: 15 minutes
THE SETUP and
GAME in PLAY

• Three heap players from each team take a place on the wave line.

• One of the two team's Front Riders takes the wave and claims priority over that wave for their team.

• If priority isn't claimed in first five minutes by the team in turn, it switches to the opposing team.

• The team with priority has each player after the Front Rider take the wave at their opportune time. The Middle Rider will follow the Front Rider onto the wave, then the Wing Man or Wild Card rider will either 'save' a play by dropping in where the Front Rider or Middle Rider lost their place or will close the play.

• The team with priority has each player after the Front Rider take the wave at their opportune time. The Middle Rider will follow the Front Rider onto the wave, then the Wing Man or Wild Card rider will either 'save' a play by dropping in where the Front Rider or Middle Rider lost their place, or will close the play.

	• When Team 1 is finished their priority time, the priority is then switched to the opposing team.
	• Players may gain points by (1) riding a wave according to rules in this rule book, (2) having more than one player from the same team on a wave at a time, (3) doing tricks on the wave, (4) doing coordinated tricks on the wave, (5) having their team stay on the wave the longest time.
	• Substitutions may be made according to the rules outlined below.

Halftime: 10 minutes

Heap 3: 15 minutes of play **THE SETUP and GAME IN PLAY**	• Three heap players from each team take a place on the wave line. • One of the two team's Front Riders takes the wave and claims priority over that wave for their team. • If priority isn't claimed in first five minutes by the team in turn, it switches to the opposing team.
	• The team with priority has each player after the Front Rider take the wave at their opportune time. The Middle Rider will follow the Front Rider onto the wave, then the Wing Man or Wild Card rider will either 'save' a play by dropping in where the Front Rider or Middle Rider lost their place or will close the play.
	• The team with priority has each player after the Front Rider take the wave at their opportune time. The Middle Rider will follow the Front Rider onto the wave, then the Wing Man or Wild Card rider will either 'save' a play by dropping in where the Front Rider or Middle Rider lost their place, or will close the play.
	• When Team 1 is finished their priority time, the priority is then switched to the opposing team.
	• Players may gain points by (1) riding a wave according to rules in this rule book, (2) having more than one player from the same team on a wave at a time, (3) doing tricks on the wave, (4) doing coordinated tricks on the wave, (5) having their team stay on the wave the longest time.
	• Substitutions may be made according to the rules outlined below.

Break - 5 minute substitution time

Heap 4: 15 minutes
THE SETUP and
GAME IN PLAY

• Three heap players from each team take a place on the wave line.

• One of the two team's Front Riders takes the wave and claims priority over that wave for their team.

• If priority isn't claimed in first five minutes by the team in turn, it switches to the opposing team.

• The team with priority has each player after the Front Rider take the wave at their opportune time. The Middle Rider will follow the Front Rider onto the wave, then the Wing Man or Wild Card rider will either 'save' a play by dropping in where the Front Rider or Middle Rider lost their place or will close the play.

• The team with priority has each player after the Front Rider take the wave at their opportune time. The Middle Rider will follow the Front Rider onto the wave, then the Wing Man or Wild Card rider will either 'save' a play by dropping in where the Front Rider or Middle Rider lost their place, or will close the play.

• When Team 1 is finished their priority time, the priority is then switched to the opposing team.

• Players may gain points by (1) riding a wave according to rules in this rule book, (2) having more than one player from the same team on a wave at a time, (3) doing tricks on the wave, (4) doing coordinated tricks on the wave, (5) having their team stay on the wave the longest time.

• Substitutions may be made according to the rules outlined below.

End of Game or Overtime

Sudden Death – Tie Breaker [If applicable]

CHAPTR 8. PLAYERS

Number of Players

Team Make Up.

This is to be determined by the league upon joining Team Wave Surfing non-profit organization. This can be a co-ed sport if stated in the member leagues submissions and bylaws.

In all cases, the preference is the OPTIMAL GAME of three heap players with a total team number of at least six and up to twelve players to represent each team, and for tie-breaking SUDDEN DEATH players.

Team Size

RULE: Team:

The TEAM WAVE SURFING league of the city or state participating has to set the GAME PLAYER NUMBER at the beginning of the season.

Optimal Game Play

1. THREE heap surfers per team
2. THREE sudden death surfers per team
3. Total number of players should be twelve with substitutions done as needed and equal play time.

Chapter 9

CHAPTER 9. DEFINITION OF TEAM AND PLAYER ROLES

Team Divisions by grade
    A. Young Riders – grade 4th to 5th
    B. Wave Riders – grade 6th to 8th
    C. High Riders - grade 9th to 12th
    D. Adult Wave Riders – this is from 18 (eighteen) years **and graduated from high school.**

Players Title and Roles for Heap
Each team has three active heap players that must work cohesively to gather the most points for their team. They are judged as a whole on how they are working together to ride the wave at one time.

Team Captain

A. TEAM CAPTAIN
(One player per team) – One of the heap players will be considered the team captain. This player will be assigned for each team before the coin toss. His/her role will be to call the coin toss and choose what priority the team will have first. This is one of the three players and may assume the role as the Front Rider, Middle Rider, or Wing Man while in the game is in play.

Heap Riders
Each team may have a total of three active players in the playing area at one time. These players will transition between the two roles. A player may take on any role during the course of the round.

B. FRONT RIDER

(Heap player) – One or more players may be the Front Rider or 'point player' by calling the wave and setting the priority for the team. The first player of the team with priority to catch the wave or one of the successions of waves within the wave line in play. He/she takes on this role when he/she commits to a wave. This individual will be judged based on the rules of the INTERNATIONAL SURFING ASSOCIATION (ISA) standards and TEAM WAVE SURFING additional point structure. Their performance will be added into the team total. Team priority is needed for a team member to be the Front Rider. He/she gains **a possible 10 points** for each wave ridden. Performance will be judged on INTERNATIONAL SURFING ASSOCIATION (ISA) governing rules on surfing competition specific to a player's performance on the surfboard (an unaffiliated party with Team Wave Surfing) in addition to ISA rules, Team Wave Surfing standards are that the player **MUST: (1) commit to wave, (2) catch and ride the wave, (3) stay steady, (4) work cohesively with their team.**

C. MIDDLE RIDER

(1) (Heap Player) - The second player of the team with priority to catch the wave or one of the successions of waves in play. This player is **any individual who is not committed to a wave**. This player comes into play after the Front Rider has committed to the priority wave. They may catch or ride any of the waves in succession on the wave line of the playing field. They will be the likely leading player to work cohesively with either the Front Rider for tricks, or the Wing Man for coordinated point capture. This player can gain additional points if they are on one of the succession of waves at the same time that the Front Rider or Wing Man are riding the wave line in play. He/she gains **a possible 10 points** for each wave ridden. Performance will be judged on ISA governing rules on surfing competition specific to a player's performance on the surfboard in addition to ISA rules, Team Wave Surfing standards are that the player **MUST: (1) commit to wave, (2) catch and ride the wave, (3) stay steady, (4) work cohesively with their team.**

D. WING MAN

(1) (Heap Player) – The final player of the team to capture one of the successions of waves in the wave line. He/she gains **a possible 10 points** for each wave ridden. This player can gain additional points if they are on one of the succession of waves at the same time that the Front Rider or Middle Rider are riding the wave line in play. Additional points can also be gained by this player if they perform a trick in cohesive play with either the Front Man or the Wing Man during their time in play. Performance for are judged on ISA governing rules on surfing competition specific to a player's performance on the surfboard in addition to ISA rules, Team Wave Surfing standards basic standards are that the player **MUST: (1) commit to wave, (2) catch and ride the wave, (3) stay steady, (4) work cohesively with their team.**

Sudden Death Tie-Breaker Round Players

Sudden death is the Tie-Breaker round. It is shorter than the heap rounds. It is only 10 minutes and played by three players from each team.

This round is only played when both teams end with the same score. The judges will call for a Sudden Death Round. The Referee will initiate the round. Sudden death has the same player positions as any other heap round.

CHAPTR 10. THE RULES

The rules are sectioned and outlined in this section. Specific penalties are referenced at the end of the rule section.

Overarching Rule – Judging of Surfing Form and Ability

Surfing performance rules are based on the rules adhered to and documented by the International Surfing Association (ISA) with which Team Wave Surfing has no current affiliation but is an accepted judging body for the art of surfing. Their rules are referred to in the judging of the points gained by a team surfer who is on the surfboard, riding their wave during their team's priority time. Additional bonus points for Team Wave Surfing are earned based on TEAM WORK principles of cohesive team game play.

Scoring Overall

Scores by players for their individual performance will be part of the team score. There will be no distinction of individual surfers as TEAM WAVE SURFING's purpose it to highlight cohesive team play. Team scores and game winnings will determine championship ranking for end of year tournaments.

Section 1- Player Eligibility Requirements

1. **Rule:** Players must be in the proper school grade and age range to play on a team.
2. **Rule:** Players must pass a swimming test to play on a team.

Penalty: Any player that does not meet the eligibility requirements will be ejected from the game and will fall under penalty 1.1

Section 2 - Player Equipment and Attire Requirements

1. **Rule:** Each player must have their own equipment as per the player equipment

listed in this document.
2. **Rule:** Each player (below the age of 16) must wear a life vest.
3. **Rule:** Each player must wear a jersey with a unique and assigned, registered number with the judges.
4. **Rule:** All team members must have the same colored jersey.
5. **Rule:** No two team members may have the same numbered jersey, and that jersey number must be reported to the judges at the beginning of the heap. Once the heap starts, jerseys cannot be switched.
6. **Rule:** Competing teams should not have the same color jersey.

Penalty: Any violation of rules 2 or 3 will result in ejection from the heap and the loss of those players' potential points. The remaining players will play, but only to gain the optimal points for two players instead of three. For other rules, substitutions can be made, but at the loss of a total of 2 team points per infraction.

Section 3 - Game Play Requirements

1. **Rule:** Each team must have three players on the wave line at a time, unless injury has occurred. In that case, they must substitute a player or forfeit the game.

Penalty: If a team has more than three players on the field, then they will be considered offside. This is a boundary foul and under penalty 2.1

2. **Rule:** The heaps will be 15 minutes long with a minimum break of 2 minutes between heaps.
3. **Rule:** Priority has to be claimed by the team that has the turn to select wave for priority within the first 5 minutes of game play time that is 15 minutes, it automatically switches to the selection of the opposing team, giving the opposing team the opportunity to go in turn, and the team with the original turn forfeits their heap round.

Penalty: The team whose turn it is to select the priority wave, must do so within the first 5 minutes of the 15 minutes of game play time or forfeit their play and potential points under penalty 2.5

4. **Rule:** The teams have the duration of the heap to score as many points as they can.

5. Rule: The Coin Toss is called by the Referee before the start of the game. The team captain that wins decides if they will have first priority at the start of the game.

6. Rule: First priority will switch between teams each heap after the first play where the winner of the coin toss identifies their team's priority.

7. Rule: All team members present for the game must play at least one heap during the game unless they are injured.

Penalty: Violation of this rule will result in an automatic loss for the team as described in penalty 1.2

8. Rule: Teams must play within the buoys in the designated game area.

Penalty: If a player goes beyond the designated game area then priority will be automatically switched to the opposing team. Any points made outside of the boundary are disregarded. The player is out of bounds and these fouls result in penalty 2.3

9. Rule: A player must not interfere with another player's ability to catch a wave or achieve points while on their wave.

Penalty: If a player makes contact with an opposing team member, then the player will be suspended for the duration of the heap as defined under penalty 3.2

10. Rule: Players may not make contact with opposing team members while they are in water and not in play during the other team's priority time.

Penalty: If a player makes contact with an opposing team member, then the player will be suspended for the rest of the heap as defined under penalty 3.1

11. Rule: There must be a lifeguard on duty during the game.

12. Rule: There must be a referee on duty during the game.

13. Rule: There must be at least three judges, but the head judge cannot be from either team.

14. Rule: The coaches cannot be in the line of play while the heap competition play is action. They have to be behind the play wave line.

15. Rule: The tie breaker and 'sudden death' round is called by the Head Judge.

16. Rule: Any protest must be submitted to the Head Judge in writing with forms available in the judge's area.

Section 4- Wave Time

1. **Rule:** The wave time must be kept for each team and reset at the end of each heap.
2. **Rule:** The wave time is calculated as the amount of time a team member is on a wave within the wave playing line. If more than one player from a team is on a wave at the same time, then the wave time should reflect both player's time on the wave.

Section 5 – Priority

1. **Rule:** A player may commit to any wave when their team has priority.
2. **Rule:** When a team does not have priority, a player on that team may only commit to a wave if they do not prevent any of the opposing team from scoring on that wave. Ex) obstructions, dropping in, etc.

Penalty: If a player's team does not have priority and interferes with the other team's ability to catch that same wave, then the priority is given to the other team and all points made during the infraction are disregarded.

3. **Rule:** Once a player commits to a wave, then the priority switches to the other team.
4. **Rule:** If a team has priority, then that team must have one player commit to a wave every two minutes.

Penalty: If a player from the team with the priority does not commit to a wave after two minutes, then priority is given to the opposing team. This team has made a wave clock violation and this foul results in penalty 2.4.

Section 6 – Substitutions

1. **Rule:** A coach must inform the referee of a substitution and get a brief approval before substituting their player.
2. **Rule:** When team is subbing out, the player in the water must go out of bounds before the replacement player can go in bounds.
3. **Rule:** Substitutions can be made during a heap, but there will be a loss of time since the team play clock doesn't stop for substitutions.
4. **Rule:** Substitutions can be made between heaps within the allotted time for the

break in heaps.

Section 7 – Scoring

1. **Rule:** A player can gain a total of **ten points** for each wave he or she rides. The

points gained are an average of the points given for that wave by judges.

2. **Rule:** There can be **two points** added to a team's score for each player that is on a wave during the same time. A minimum of two players from the same team must be up on a wave at the same time.

3. **Rule:** A **ten point** bonus at the end of each heap will be added to the team total of the team with the highest wave time and the highest number of players in play until the end. If both teams have three players in play until the end, they both earn the bonus points.

Section 8 - Unsafe Conditions

1. **Rule:** If the surfer's board is lost during team play, time stops, board caddy (another surfer not the players in play) can retrieve the board. The team holds the points accumulated. If board can't be recovered, another player can substitute.

2. **Rule:** If surfer notes danger they must signal to referee, and referee calls time. No substitutions or play can be made until lifeguard and Head Judge affirm conditions are safe to continue play. After approval to play is granted, the team starts with the surfers who haven't played. Time will stop during the assessment.

3. **Rule:** The Head Judge may call the game to a premature end at any time in the occurrence of unforeseen issues such as weather, water conditions, etc. The final score will be calculated and recorded at that time, if more than half the game has been played. If less than half of the game has been played then the game is not recorded and may be rescheduled.

Section 9 - Sudden Death

1. **Rule:** In the case of a tie, a 5 minute sudden death heap will be added to the end of the game.

2. **Rule:** Before a sudden death heap starts, a coin toss is called by the Referee. The team captain that wins decides if they will have first priority for the sudden death heap.

3. **Rule:** During sudden death, if a team has priority, then that team must have one player commit to a wave **every minute**.

Penalty: If a player from the team with the priority does not commit to a wave after one minute, then priority is given to the opposing team. This team has made a wave clock violation and this foul results in penalty 2.4

Equipment for playing Team Wave Surfing

A. Equipment Per Player
1. Surfboard: long, thick, wide board
2. Life vest: for safety it is required for all kids under 16, players 16 and older can sign waiver to refuse the requirement to wear life vest.

B. Equipment Per Game
1. Air horn: for announcing surfing play time start and end times
2. Timer: for timing heaps, breaks, and wave time
3. Buoys: to designate the surf zones
4. Binoculars: for use by the referees and judges
5. Score board: for scorekeeping
6. Bull horn: for announcing by referee or judges
7. Stopwatch: for keeping track of time on waves
8. Megaphone: to announce gameplay
9. Cones: for team bench designation
10. Tables: for scoreboard
11. Tent for scorekeeping and timekeeping

Player Eligibility
1. AGE: 10 years old at the start of the team season
2. SKILL: Must be able to swim and pass the team swim test
3. SKILL: Must be comfortable with the water and able to carry their own surfboard

Team Registration and Leagues
TEAM LEAGUES should be registered with the TEAM WAVE SURFING Organization. The approval process would include the team and the league having:

A. League registration and eligibility
1. Proof of Insurance – each league must have sports insurance paid and up to date before registration.

At least four teams registered – each league must have at least four teams in its umbrella with the minimum number of players expected.

2. Registration of Coaches – after (1) Proof of Insurance, (2) Identification of teams, the league is expected to provide:

The list of their coaches.

3. Proof of criminal background checks on coaches, team moms, assistants.

4. Practice location approvals – the league is expected to provide permits, approvals, and proof of scheduled practice locations.

5. Game location approvals – the league is expected to provide permits, approvals and proof of scheduled game locations.

6. Tournament location approvals – the league is expected to provide permits, approvals, and proof of scheduled tournament locations.

B. Team Wave Surfing Non-Profit organization will provide:

1. Officials for games where applicable.
2. Referees.
3. Yearly Tournaments.
4. Rule Book.
5. Oversight.

Leagues

The development of leagues must adhere to the standards and rules of the locality and place of play or engagement. The approval and membership through Team Wave Surfing for rulebook and oversight of the sport is expected to be completed prior to league season start.

Youth Leagues

Youth leagues should be vetted through Team Wave Surfing Non-Profit organization to validate that the league agrees to adhere to the safety of the players, the positive presence of the sport, and to receive charter.

Adult Leagues

College and adult leagues are anticipated in the future.

CHAPTER 11. PENALTIES

The accumulation of any penalties will result in a change of priority to the opposing team of the team in violation. During the referee's resolution of any foul, all game play must cease. Any points gathered during this time, or during the time of the foul, will be disregarded.

The penalty severity is decided upon by the Head Judge after a referee calls the penalty.

Section 1 - Individual and Team Violations

1. Penalty 1.1: Violations will result in ejection of the player from the game. The player will not be allowed back into the game once ejected. The player will be suspended from all future games unless given a written exception by the league.
2. Penalty 1.2: Violations will result in automatic loss for the violating team. Game will be reviewed and if violation did occur, then game will be recorded as a loss.
3. Penalty 1.3: Violations will result in ejection from the heap. The player will not be allowed back into the game until the heap in which the violation occurred is complete. The player may compete in the next heap if the violation is resolved.

Section 2 - Minor Gameplay Violations

1. Penalty 2.1: Violations will result in the removal of the extra player from the game. The clock will stop while the player exits the playing area. The game will continue once the team is without violation. Any points that the team made while in violation will be disregarded.
2. Penalty 2.2: Player in violation must move at least 20 yards from player that

infraction was made upon. The opposing team is given two consecutive priorities. Once player is 20 yards away, the game may continue upon the referee's signal.

3. Penalty 2.3: Player in violation must move back into the playing area and game may continue upon the referee's signal.

4. Penalty 2.4: Priority is changed to the opposing team. The game may continue upon the referee's signal.

5. Penalty 2.5: If player on team with choice of priority doesn't commit to a wave within the wave line in the first 5 minutes of play of the 15 minutes of HEAP time, they forfeit their turn and potential of points for the specified Heap.

Section 3 - Major Gameplay Offenses

1. Penalty 3.1: Violations will result in the violating player's immediate removal and suspension from the game. Player will not be allowed to re-enter the game. **Three of these offenses made by a team will result in an automatic loss.**

2. Penalty 3.2: Violations will result in the violating player's removal from the heap. The player will not be allowed back in the heap where the infraction occurred. The player may enter the next heap. If a single player gains two penalties then he or she will be suspended for the rest of the game.

Double Fouls

1. In the case where a foul is committed by a player of each team during the same time, a coin toss will be initiated with the team captains to determine who has first priority. A single team captain will call the coin toss and the team that wins will have first priority.

2. If two different players from the same team commit a foul simultaneously, then the penalties for each foul must handled.

3. If the same player commits two or more fouls simultaneously, then the following shall apply:

4. If foul is a section 1 foul, all penalties will be dealt out.

5. If foul does not have a section 1 penalty, only one penalty is dealt. The penalty with higher priority will be dealt. The priority goes to the higher penalty number.

Chapter 12

CHAPER 12. COMPETITION GAME RULES AND PROCEDURES

OFFICIATORS

A. REFEREE –

There must be at least 1 referee but up to two.

- Signals when rule violations occur
- Ensures all penalties are carried out
- Facilitates gameplay

B. HEAD JUDGE –

There is only one head judge.

- Announces the winner
- Tallies the points
- Notes penalty point removals

C. JUDGES –

There should be at least one other judge that watches for points, penalties and forfeits.

D. SCORE KEEPERS –

There should be at least one that helps judges keep track of points and sends points to head judge for validation.

E. TIME KEEPERS –

There should be at least one that times and announces:

- Coin Toss
- The start of Surf Off for the team in play

- The end of the heap or sudden death match

F. WAVE TIME KEEPER —

There should be at least one person that keeps track of the amount of time each team had a player on a wave. This person must total each team's time at the end of each heap.

G. LIFEGUARDS –

There should be at least two lifeguards. One per team.

H. INFORMER –

Sends communication from Lifeguard, Referee, Head Judge and coaches and is the only other officiator that can go back and forth out of game play area.

I. FLAGGER —

There should be at least one person that holds colored flags to indicate which team has the priority. This individual may also be a time keeper.

Chapter 13

CHAPTR 13. TIME IN GAME

A. COIN TOSS – The game begins with a coin toss between Team Captains. 1 minute to toss and select winner.

- Winner of Toss – gets to decide to go first in the game.

B. DURATION OF THE GAME – The game plays for four heaps of 15 minutes and an optional final sudden death match of 5 minutes. The total play time should be 45 minutes plus three 2-minute heap breaks and halftime of 10 minutes.

C. STARTING CLOCK – The timekeeper manages the starting clock and that is when the team's 15-minute heap time, or 5-minute sudden death time is in play.

- **Begins After** (1) Coin Toss, (2) Referee's signal for the heap to begin.

D. WAVE TIME – The wave time keeper must keep a running total of the time each team has a member on the wave. A team's total is to be reported then reset at the end of each heap.

- **Time deductions**: Please note any penalties accumulated can potentially deduct wave time score.

E. BETWEEN HEAP TIME – Each team has two minutes to make substitutions between heaps and have all players within the playing area before the continuation of the game.

F. BOUNDARIES OF GAME – Takes place within the buoy lines within the wave.

CHAPTER 14. POINTS EARNINGS

Heap Points

A. HEAP POINTS – Are gained during the 15-minute heaps.

1. (Up to) Ten points per player for adherence to form and rules set by the ISA judging rules (unaffiliated party).

- Surf performance score per player on the team while on the surf board is judged on criteria set forth by the ISA (unaffiliated party).
- Final wave score is an average of the judges' scores for that wave based on ISA judging rules. It is added for each player and is the team score.
- No player holds an individual score. Their score is added to the other two players in play for the total score for the team in the specified heap.

—Additional two points for each player from the same

- a. Team that rides a wave at the same time as another team player.
- b. Minimum of two players must being riding a wave at the same time to gain additional points.
- c. Minimum of 4 additional points can be awarded with a maximum of 6 additional points.

2. Three points will be awarded at the end of each heap to the team that has the longest wave riding time.

- Each team has a running total of the length of time a team member was on a wave.

- Total wave time is kept for each heap then reset at the end of the heap.
- Their wave time is captured and any penalty time is subtracted from their overall wave time bonus score potential.

3. Five points will be awarded to the team that has the most team members (2 or more) on the wave at the end of the team in play time.

4. Five points bonus points will be awarded at the end of each heap to the team that has all three players on the wave at the end of the team in play time.

Tie Breaker Points

B. TIE BREAKER - SUDDEN DEATH POINTS **[used for TIE BREAKER ONLY]**

In cases where both teams have the same amount of points, a SUDDEN DEATH tie breaker round can be called by:
- Head Judge
- Referee with Head Judge approval

1. **(Up to) ten points** for each wave caught by a player.
   - Wave is judged on criteria set forth by the ISA (unaffiliated party).
   - Final wave score is an average of the judges' scores for that wave.

—**Additional two points** for each player from the same team that rides a wave at the same time.
   - Minimum of two players must being riding a wave at the same time to gain additional points
   - Minimum of 4 additional points can be awarded with a maximum of 6 additional points

2. No points will be awarded for the team with the highest wave time, but team inactivity violations will be enacted.

CHAPTER 15. TEAM IN PLAY

Coin Toss

- **COIN TOSS** – Start of game with coin toss between team captains. One minute to toss and select winner.

Start of the game

- **Surf Off** – An air horn sounds to signal start and end of heaps. Starts when the horn from the timekeeper is blown. The team in play is the only team on the wave.

Keeping of time

1. **Time Keeper** – Announce when each player has finished their requirement of:
   - 5-minute player set up time
   - 5-minutes for priority to be claimed by the team in play or they forfeit their play time for the heap.
   - 15-minute end of heap
   - 10-minute end of sudden death
   - 10-minute halftime
   - 5-minute point tallying by judges
   - Time out (although there are no scheduled time outs, these are timed and the **air horn** sounds when the time is up)

   2. Team In Play – Captures as many points as possible during the heap and if there is a tie, then the sudden death heap.

3. Halt of game – Happens when Referee notes a violation, removes points, injury of a player, lifeguard call to referee, or calls forfeited on heap or sudden death round.

4. Substitutions – Can only be done during the heap with the referee's approval, or when there is a PLAYER INJURY.

5. Scoring Display – This is done after each heap and sudden death. The points are calculated and displayed at the judge's table for the teams.

BETWEEN HEAP BREAKS –
Players have two minutes to switch out and re-enter the playing area between heaps.

SCORING –
Is displayed at the judge's table, is tallied at the end of each heap, and announced by the Head Judge.

RESTARTS –
This happens only when there is an injury or a penalty.
- CLOCK STARTS from the time the IN PLAY heap or sudden death time stop. It is the REMAINING time in play.

TIME OUTS – There are no time outs, with the exception of INJURY.
- Injury: in which teams resume once the player is safely transported to shore
- Lifeguard call: When lifeguard notes an emergency or danger by **2 honks** on air horn

SUBSTITUTIONS – Can be made during the heap with the referee's approval or between heaps.

SUDDEN DEATH (Tie breaker only) – Is the final round of the 5 rounds total. There are 4 heaps, with each team having 2 heaps to perform, and the final round, is a head-to-head sudden death round of three players from each team to gain additional points to break the tie score.

Out of Bounds

OUT OF BOUNDS MARK OR OFF SIDES:

OUT OF BOUNDS –
When a player goes beyond the BUOYs that are placed as the game play boundaries.

OFF WAVE LINE –

When more than three players from the same team are in the playing area at any time during the heap.

Procedural Violations

- Team Interference: If team interferes with opposing team's game play, the team forfeits priority at the time of the call, and the team affected will receive 2 points per player affected.
- Offshore misconduct: Results in the suspension of player from the remainder of the game and all of the players earned points for that game shall be disregarded.

Misconduct

SUSPENSIONS

- Lewd or rude behavior to opposing team, judges, referee, or guest will result in disqualification of player and penalty to team.
- PROTESTS will be communicated through coach to the head judge.

Injuries

INJURIES – called by the lifeguard

Suspended Games

- SUSPENDED GAMES – called by the Head Judge

Forfeits

FORFEITS

If team has less than 2 players to participate in any heap the team will be deemed unfit to perform and forfeit the game.

Exception:

- If team has minimal players and loses a player due to injury they are allowed to finish game with at least 2 players minimum. This rule does not apply when a player is ejected from the game as caused by a penalty.
- If a team does not show up to participate after 20 minutes have transpired since the scheduled start of the game, then the team automatically forfeits.

Rule Book

RULE BOOKS PER TEAM

One rule book is supplied per team. It will have the year's rules and addendums within it.

AWARDS

The awards will be earned on basis of the member league and chartered member's participation in Team Wave Surfing final championship tournament.

Mediation

- The commissioner of the league serves as mediator between teams.
- TEAM WAVE SURFING MEDIATION COORDINATOR is involved if the teams aren't in agreement with the league commissioner.

Chapter 16

CHAPTER 16. JUDGING

Judges will evaluate player's maneuvers based on the guidelines set forth by the International Surfing Association (ISA) which is an unaffiliated body who is an acceptable guideline for judging surf form and ability. Each player will be judged individually, but points will be totaled for the team at the end of each heat.

Point deductions should be made individually and applied to the team total. Bonus points for the team wave time should be calculated and added at the end of each heap.

The judging in this team sport is different than judging solo surfer specified sports. Each player is judged individually, but the their points work towards the team's total. Additional heat points and point deductions are made based on overall team performance.

— Considerations when judging:
1. Amount of time player rides the wave
2. Maneuvers completed during ride time
3. Player activity away from the wave
4. Deductions when bypassing wave priority
5. Priority shifts due to team inactivity

ABOUT TEAM WAVE SURFING

Team Wave Surfing is a new sport on the sport of surfing. It's an interactive game between two teams who gain points for traditional surfing techniques when playing as one team of three players on the wave line to gain points for their cohesive game play. This rule book shares the creation of the game, how to play the game and the judging of the game. Team Wave Surfing was created to offer an opportunity for youth to play together, work together while surfing to introduce a new spin on the sport of surfing.

ABOUT THE TEAM WAVE SURFING ORGANIZATION

Team wave surfing's non-profit organization has a mission to support and promote the sport of team wave surfing. As the sport's national governing body, Team Wave Surfing provides leadership, structure, and resources to fuel the sport's growth and enrich the experience of participants.

The organization is in charge of publishing, distributing, and editing for the Team Wave Surfing Rule Book. Improvements to the books will be made based on the needs of those involved in the sport and distributed freely to the leagues. The Team Wave Surfing Non-Profit Organization will provide assistance in setting up new leagues, oversight for all for participating leagues, and national competitions.

TURNING SURFING INTO A TEAM SPORT

www.teamwavesurfing.org

* * *

www.ingramcontent.com/pod-product-compliance
Lightning Source LLC
Chambersburg PA
CBHW080534030426
42337CB00023B/4723